D0909315

# Mysterious Encounters

# Burial Grounds

## by Rachel Lynette

**KIDHAVEN PRESS**
*A part of Gale, Cengage Learning*

GALE
CENGAGE Learning™

Detroit • New York • San Francisco • New Haven, Conn • Waterville, Maine • London

© 2010 Gale, Cengage Learning

LIBRARY OF CONGRESS CATALOGING-IN-PUBLICATION DATA

Lynette, Rachel.
  Burial grounds / by Rachel Lynette.
      p. cm. -- (Mysterious encounters)
  Includes bibliographical references and index.
  ISBN 978-0-7377-4411-8 (hardcover)
  1. Cemeteries--Juvenile literature. 2. Tombs--Juvenile literature. I. Title.
  GT3320.L96 2009
  363.7'5--dc22
                                                                        2009022094

KidHaven Press
27500 Drake Rd.
Farmington Hills, MI 48331

ISBN-13: 978-0-7377-4411-8
ISBN-10: 0-7377-4411-1

Printed in the United States of America
1 2 3 4 5 6 7 13 12 11 10 09

Printed by Bang Printing, Brainerd, MN 1st Ptg., 08/2009

# Contents

# Chapter 1

# Home of the Dead

*Remember me, as you pass by,*
*As you are now, so once was I,*
*As I am now, so you must be*
*Prepare for death and follow me.*

This **epitaph** has been engraved on many tombstones. It is a reminder to all who see it that everyone dies eventually. When a person dies, it is up to the living to take care of the dead person's body. Bodies are usually **cremated** or buried in a cemetery. The word *cemetery* comes from a Greek word meaning "to sleep."

## Why Bury the Dead?

People bury the dead for many reasons. From a

practical standpoint, it is a quick and easy way to dispose of a dead body. Once a person dies, his or her body begins to decompose. This means the body decays, or rots. A decomposing body is very unpleasant to smell and it attracts maggots and other insects. For these reasons, it is important that bodies are buried promptly. It is also important to bury a body quickly if the person died of a **contagious** disease. Contagious diseases can spread from dead bodies to living people.

People in many cultures believe that burying a person's body is a way to show respect for the person who died. Most people feel that a burial is more dignified and respectful than leaving the body out in the open to decompose. A burial ceremony can

Watching the burial of a loved one can help bring closure for family and friends.

also bring comfort to family and friends and help them understand and accept the finality of death, so they can move on with their lives.

Burial customs are different for different religions and cultures. Some customs were established because of fear of the dead. The practice of covering the head with a sheet may come from the belief that the spirit can escape through the mouth to haunt the living. In ancient times, the Saxons of England sometimes cut the feet off a **corpse** so that it could not follow the living. Other customs are based on showing respect for the dead. Jewish customs require that a body be buried no more than two nights after death. In the past, Christians buried their dead with the feet toward the East because they believed in a judgment day when the body would be **resurrected**. It was thought that the resurrection would come from the East.

## A Graveyard for Every Body

There are many ways to bury the dead. In some cultures the dead are buried close to the living—even in the yard or under the house. In other cultures they are buried far away. Wealthy and important people are often given elaborate burials, while a criminal might simply be tossed into a pit.

During the Middle Ages, most of the people in Europe were very religious. They believed that burial under a church or in a churchyard would increase their chances of getting into heaven. However, this soon became a problem as there was a lim-

Many believed that burial in a churchyard meant they would get into heaven.

ited amount of space. Diseases like bubonic plague and smallpox often killed many people in a short period of time. It soon became clear that the dead would have to be buried somewhere else. Large pits were dug outside villages for the victims of these diseases.

The first planned cemeteries, sometimes called garden cemeteries, were created outside of towns. Usually they were designed to have a parklike setting with trees, pathways, and monuments for the dead. These types of cemeteries tend to have a peaceful

## Suicide in the Middle Ages

In the Middle Ages if a person committed suicide, their body was not allowed to be buried in the churchyard. Instead, the body was buried in an unmarked grave in an area surrounded by a fence with no gate. This meant that the body had to be lifted over the fence to complete the burial process and visitors were rare.

feeling. They are also very interesting, containing many different kinds of monuments honoring the dead. Some plots are marked with statues, elaborately carved headstones, benches, or other decorations, while others are marked with a small stone or a simple wooden cross. These cemeteries are often divided into sections for members of the same family, or of the same religious or cultural group. Some of the oldest cemeteries, especially those that are neglected, are thought to be haunted.

Another kind of cemetery is a military cemetery. Military cemeteries are reserved for current members of the military, eligible **veterans**, and certain family members of the **deceased**. Many military cemeteries were created during the American Civil War (1861–1865). Most of these are located near hospitals or battlegrounds. Gettysburg National Military Park in Gettysburg, Pennsylvania, is one of the larger cemeteries. Thousands of soldiers lost their lives in the three-day-long Battle of Gettysburg in 1863. Today people often claim to see ghosts among the graves, reenacting the final moments of their lives.

Recently, cemeteries have taken the form of memorial parks. Unlike garden cemeteries, memorial parks do not have elaborate monuments, headstones, or landscaping. Instead, the grave markers are flat, making it possible to mow right over them. These cemeteries are designed to be easy to care for.

Cemeteries are not just for people. There are also pet cemeteries where people can have their beloved companions buried. Pet cemeteries welcome the bodies of dogs, cats, birds, snakes, hamsters, even

One of the best-known military cemeteries is Arlington National Cemetery in Washington DC.

## Storing Bodies

**Digging a grave when the ground is frozen is not an easy task. That is why bodies in Alaska are often stored during the winter for burial in the spring. In Anchorage, 100 bodies can be stored in a refrigerated cooler. When the ground thaws, the bodies are buried.**

llamas and potbellied pigs. The Los Angeles Pet Memorial Park is home to the remains of pets that belonged to movie stars. Animal ghosts have been reported. The most frequent is a Great Dane named Kabar. Kabar belonged to Rudolph Valentino, a famous actor in the early 1900s. It is said that Kabar appears near his grave and licks the hands of those who pass.

## Visiting a Cemetery

Many people who visit cemeteries do so to visit the grave of a loved one. Others come to look at interesting or historic grave markers or simply to enjoy the parklike setting. Many cemeteries offer pamphlets with information and even maps showing where certain people are buried. Professional ghost hunters sometimes visit cemeteries with cameras and special equipment to detect paranormal activity.

In addition to cemeteries, people also visit the

The head of this gravestone has been knocked off by cemetery vandals.

burial grounds of ancient cultures. **Archaeologists** carefully excavate ancient burial grounds. A great deal can be learned about a culture's way of life and religious beliefs by studying the way its people buried their dead. Many of these sites are now protected and are open to the public.

# Chapter 2

# Ancient Burials

Archaeologists study ancient grave sites to learn more about the people who are buried there. Often, however, what they find leaves them with more questions than answers. Ancient burial customs usually revolved around a culture's beliefs and superstitions about death. When an archaeologist excavates a grave site, it is his or her job to determine what those beliefs might be. For example, a burial ground in Colombia contains the remains of a woman who some archaeologists think was buried alive as a human sacrifice. According to archaeologist Ana Maria Groot, "her mouth is open as if in terror, and her hands seem contracted as if she had tried grabbing hold of something."[1] However, another archaeologist notes that her mouth may be open because of how she was moved and her hands could be contracted due to early arthritis. Did this ancient culture have beliefs that entailed burying people alive or was this woman simply a victim of arthritis? For now at least, the answer remains a mystery.

## The Mound Builders

After examining ancient tombs, archaeologists **theorize** about the people who built them. Sometimes the **theories** turn out to be completely wrong. When explorers came to the New World over 500 years ago, they found many large, mysterious mounds in the earth that were clearly man-made. The mounds were in the shapes of pyramids with flat tops, cones, and ridges and in geometric shapes, like squares and octagons. Some were even shaped like animals. Early excavations yielded human bones along with objects, such as tools, jewelry, statues, pipes, and shells.

At the time, most of the European settlers did not believe the native people were organized and advanced enough to have built the mounds. Instead they believed the mounds were built by an advanced race of people who had mysteriously vanished. There were many theories about who these people might have been. Clergyman and scholar Ezra Stiles asserted that the mounds were built by the Canaanites who, according to the Bible, were expelled from Palestine by Joshua. Inventor

The Serpent Mound in Ohio was built by Native Americans over 90 years ago.

and colonist Benjamin Franklin thought they were built by the Spanish explorer Hernando de Soto. Naturalist Benjamin Smith Barton argued that the mounds were the tombs of Vikings. Another popular idea was that the mounds were built by the ten lost tribes of Israel. For over 100 years archaeologists, scientists, and even novelists continued to come up with ideas about who the unknown people might be.

There was one colonist, Thomas Jefferson, who

examined the mounds and stated that they were built by the ancestors of present-day Native Americans. Although he was ignored at the time, it turns out he was correct. By the early 1900s, stories of a mysterious advanced race had died out in favor of Jefferson's simple and correct explanation.

## City of the Dead

Even when archaeologists can determine who built a tomb, there may still be many unanswered questions. Such is the case with the Mausoleum of the First Qin Emperor.

# Tomb Robbers in Ancient China

**Despite the fact that many of the laborers who worked on Emperor Shih Huang Ti's tomb were executed to keep them from revealing the tomb's secrets, some scientists believe that the tomb was probably robbed shortly after he was buried. Other scientists argue that the large quantities of mercury reported to be in the tomb would have killed anyone who tried to enter it.**

In 1974 farmers digging a well in Northwest China made one of the most important archaeological discoveries ever. They had dug about 13 feet (4m) when they discovered a life-size human figure constructed from **terra-cotta**. The figure was a soldier and is the first of what archaeologists believe is an army of 8,000 terra-cotta soldiers constructed to guard the tomb of the first emperor of China, Shih Huang Ti.

Shih Huang Ti became emperor in 221 B.C. when he was just thirteen years old. He started construction on his tomb almost immediately, and it was still not finished 36 years later when he died

Hundreds of terra-cotta warriors found in Emperor Shih Huang Ti's tomb.

suddenly of a mysterious illness. More than a tomb, the emperor had ordered the construction of an entire underground city, complete with a palace, temples, stables, music halls, parks, and even a cemetery. Shih Huang Ti was an effective, though cruel ruler. His elaborate underground city was paid for by the taxes of peasants and built by 700,000 slaves and prisoners. The emperor was afraid of death and historians believe he had the tomb constructed so that he could live forever in the spirit world.

It is thought that Shih Huang Ti is buried in the palace, along with workers who were unfortunate enough to be in the tomb when the gates were closed. Historian Sima Qian wrote about the construction and contents of the palace one hundred years after the emperor's death:

> They [workers] dug through three subterranean streams and poured molten copper for the outer coffin, and the tomb was filled with models of palaces, pavilions and offices as well as fine vessels, precious stones and rarities. Artisans were ordered to fix up crossbows so that any thief breaking in would be shot. All the country's streams, the Yellow River and the Yangtze were reproduced in quicksilver [mercury] and by some mechanical means made to flow into a miniature ocean. The heavenly constellations were above and the regions of the earth below. The candles were made of

whale oil to insure the burning for the longest possible time.[2]

Could the emperor's tomb really contain so many riches and even be protected by booby-trapped crossbows? For now, these questions are unanswered. The Chinese government decided not to excavate the tomb because it believes that excavating it will destroy it. "These cultural relics have been buried in the tomb for more than 1,000 years. If they are excavated and exposed to sunlight, oxygen or other gases, they will change immediately,"[3] said Zhang Bai, deputy director of the State Bureau of Cultural Relics.

## The Mummy's Curse

Like Emperor Shih Huang Ti, the rulers, or pharaohs, of ancient Egypt also believed in an afterlife,

A view of King Tutankhamen's tomb and its elaborate wall paintings.

which is why they constructed the giant pyramids that became their tombs. Pharaohs were buried with food, furniture, weapons, sporting equipment, treasures, and even servants—everything they would need to be happy in the afterlife.

Although there are many Egyptian tombs, the most well-known is that of King Tutankhamen, also known as King Tut. Historians do not believe King Tut was a particularly important king when he was alive. He became a pharaoh when he was just nine years old and only ruled for about ten years before he died. However, unlike most of the other pharaohs' tombs, King Tut's tomb was found nearly undisturbed. Other tombs had been robbed and vandalized, leaving little for archaeologists to discover thousands of years later.

King Tut's tomb was first opened by archaeologist Howard Carter on November 26, 1922. Lord Carnarvon, the English nobleman who was funding Carter's efforts was also present. The tomb was filled with amazing **artifacts** and treasures. News of the discovery made headlines around the world. Some reporters wrote that the mummy of King Tut was cursed because Carter had found a stone tablet inscribed with the words "death will slay with his wings whoever disturbs the peace of the pharaoh."[4] Carter denied that the tablet existed and one was never found. The rumors of a curse might have disappeared had Lord Carnarvon not fallen ill from blood poisoning from an infected mosquito bite.

While Carnarvon lay dying, Marie Corelli, a popular novelist, warned that "the most dire punishment follows any rash intruder into the sealed tomb."[5] Carnarvon died just two weeks later. It was said that all of the lights in Cairo, Egypt, went out at the moment of his death. Further, there were reports that Carnarvon's beloved dog, still in England, began to howl and then died, just as his master did thousands of miles away.

Many artifacts, such as this ceremonial shield, were found in King Tut's tomb.

Over the next ten years, eleven people associated with the tomb died early of unnatural causes. By 1935, the count had risen to 21. The papers covered each new death in great detail and belief in the mummy's curse grew.

Although many people believed in the curse, there were also many who did not. Skeptics point out that Carnarvon was 57 years old and in poor health before he was even bitten by the mosquito. Further, although some people did die, most of the workers, archaeologists, and others involved in the excavation did not. Carter himself lived to the age of 66 and died of natural causes. Scientists suggest that ancient mold from inside the tomb could have been the real killer. German microbiologist Gotthard Kramer has found mold spores on 40 mummies. "When spores enter the body through the nose, mouth or eye mucous membranes, they can lead to organ failure or even death, particularly in individuals with weakened immune systems,"[6] says Kramer.

# Chapter 3

# Haunted Graveyards

Many ancient cultures believed that a person's spirit lived on after the death of the body. Most cultures also believed that disturbing the spirits of the dead was not a good idea and could result in injury and even death for the living. Today, many people still believe that restless spirits haunt the places where their bodies are buried. People often report hearing or seeing these spirits, also known as ghosts, though thankfully, few report being injured by them.

## Resurrection Mary

One of the most well-known ghost stories takes

Resurrection Mary is often seen on the road by the cemetery or within the cemetery itself.

place on a road that runs past Resurrection Cemetery in Chicago, Illinois. According to the story, a young woman attended a dance with her boyfriend in the early 1930s. The girl was beautiful; she had blond hair and pale skin. She wore a white dress. At some point during the evening, she had a fight with her boyfriend. Rather than allowing him to drive her home, she decided to hitchhike. She never made it home. While walking along the side of the road, she was hit by a car. The driver did not stop, but instead sped off, leaving the girl to die alone.

Haunted Graveyards    **25**

The girl was buried in her white dress in Resurrection Cemetery. It was not long after her burial that she started appearing to motorists driving along the road that runs by the cemetery gates. She is most often seen on cold and rainy nights, always wearing her white dress. She appears to be real to those who see her. In many stories, the passing driver stops to give her a ride. Although the driver tries to engage her in conversation, she talks very little. She always insists on being dropped off at the gates of the cemetery. Often, she simply disappears from the car. Other times, she gets out of the car and disappears just before she gets to the gates.

In other stories, the girl, who has come to be known as Resurrection Mary, does not hitch a ride. Instead she suddenly appears in the road in front of

## Who Was Resurrection Mary?

Although many claim to have seen Resurrection Mary, no one has been able to connect the ghost to a real person. There are no records of a girl in Resurrection Cemetery who died while hitchhiking. Some people believe that Mary is simply an urban legend with no basis in fact.

a moving car. When the horrified driver hits her, she disappears. Perhaps the most frightening story about Resurrection Mary occurred on August 10, 1976. Around 10:30 at night a driver saw a girl in a white dress standing behind the gate of the cemetery. She was grasping the bars of the gate and appeared to have been locked in at closing time. The driver alerted the police, but when the officer arrived, the girl was gone. However, the officer did find evidence of Mary's presence. Two of the bars on the gate were bent. There were brown impressions in the bars that seemed to have come from small hands. Could the bars have been bent by Resurrection Mary?

## Voodoo Queen Marie Laveau

Unlike Resurrection Mary, Marie Laveau was famous and powerful while still alive. Marie was born in New Orleans, Louisiana, in 1794. Although her mother was a slave, her father was a wealthy plantation owner so she was born free. Marie became a hairdresser, working for the well-to-do of her community. Her clients often confided in her, gossiping and telling her their secrets. In this way she learned many secrets that she was able to use to her advantage. Marie became a practitioner of **voodoo**, holding rituals and casting spells. Many people came to her seeking power, love, or revenge on an enemy. She soon became one of the most feared and powerful people in New Orleans.

The voodoo queen's power did not end when

The tomb of voodoo queen Marie Laveau, who is thought to haunt the St. Louis Cemetery No. 1 in New Orleans.

## Sick and Tired

**Elmore Lee Banks, the man who claims to have seen the ghost of Marie Laveau in the drugstore near St. Louis Cemetery No. 1, may have been ill at the time. His illness might have caused him to hallucinate the entire event.**

she died in 1881. She was buried in a vault in St. Louis Cemetery No. 1 in New Orleans. People regularly visited her tomb, leaving gifts of money, flowers, and food and asking for her help. Drawing the letter *X* on her tomb and knocking on it three times is thought to bring her spirit forth. In addition, many have claimed to see her wandering the cemetery. Sometimes she is seen dancing or with her large snake, Zombi. Others believe she appears as a large black cat with red eyes or as a black crow.

In one story from the mid-1930s, Marie Laveau appeared in a drugstore located near the cemetery. She became angry when a customer named Elmore Lee Banks did not know who she was. She slapped Banks and, according to him, "she jump[ed] up in the air and went whizzing out the door and over the top of the telephone wires. She passed right over the graveyard wall and disappeared."[7]

# The Ghosts of Greenwood

No one knows exactly when Greenwood Cemetery in Decatur, Illinois, first became a resting place for the dead. There is evidence that Native Americans are buried there as well as early settlers of the region. The first recorded burial was in 1840. Although the cemetery was well maintained in the early 1900s, it is not cared for very well now. Parts of the cemetery have been abandoned, and vandals have destroyed many of the stones.

There are many tales of haunting at Greenwood. One of the most well-known is that of the Greenwood Bride. In the 1930s, a young woman had plans to elope with a man her parents disapproved of. Before the couple could carry out their plans, however, the man was murdered and his body was thrown into a nearby river. When the young woman

heard of the murder, she took her own life, drowning herself in the same river. Her parents found her wedding dress in her closet and blamed themselves. If they had approved of their daughter's suitor, they might both still be alive. They buried her in Greenwood, in her wedding dress. Since that time, many people have reported seeing a ghostly figure of a young woman in a glowing wedding dress wandering among the stones and crying.

The cemetery is also said to be haunted by two children. Michael is a small boy dressed in torn overalls. He is often angry and frequently pushes people or throws things at them. He has also thrown rocks at passing cars, sometimes damaging the windshield. Maggie Jane is much friendlier. She carries a doll and has been known to remove flowers from other graves to put on her own grave. People who

have brought flowers and gifts to her grave have reported hearing a voice say "thank you." In one particularly eerie story, a mother is visiting the cemetery with her baby. A young girl asks if she can play with the baby and hold him. When the mother is ready to leave, she asks the girl where her

Greenwood Cemetery in Illinois is thought to be haunted by a bride, soldiers, a boy, and a young girl named Maggie Jane.

own parents are, and the girl replies, "Well, they don't come to my grave in a long time."[8]

Near the edge of the Greenwood Cemetery lie the bodies of Confederate soldiers from the Civil War. The soldiers were prisoners bound for a camp up north. On the way many of them contracted yellow fever and died. Union soldiers hauled the bodies off the train and buried them in shallow graves. It is likely that some of the men they buried were not actually dead yet. Many people believe it is the spirits of soldiers who were buried alive that haunt the cemetery. People have reported hearing strange voices and footsteps. Some have even seen transparent soldiers. In one case, one of the soldiers talked to a young boy saying, "Can you help me? I don't know where I am and I want to go home."[9] The man disappeared before the boy could reply.

# Chapter 4

# Disturbing the Dead

People not only bury their dead as a way to dispose of the body, but also to show respect for their loved one and to create a memorial for the living. Once the dead are buried, they are expected to stay in the ground. It does not always work out that way, however. There are many reasons, both legal and illegal, to **exhume** a body.

Grave robbers dig up bodies to steal things that have been buried with them. Thieves dig up newly buried bodies to sell to medical facilities for research. People sometimes have a body exhumed to confirm that the correct body is in the grave. In some cases, bodies are exhumed in order to solve a crime. Sometimes the dead are exhumed not because people are interested in the bodies themselves, but because they are interested in the land where the bodies are buried. Bodies may be exhumed to make room for new bodies, or even for development. In these cases, the bodies must all be dug up and carefully moved to another location.

## Solving a Murder

A lot can be learned from a dead body. A medical examiner is a doctor who examines dead bodies and determines how they died. Sometimes a medical examiner decides that a person was murdered, even when it first looks like he or she died from an accident. That was exactly what happened in the case of Kathleen Savio. Savio was found dead in her bathtub in 2004. Her death appeared to be an accident. Four years later, however, police became suspicious of Kathleen Savio's husband, Drew Peterson. Peterson had remarried after Savio's death and his next wife, Stacy Peterson, was now missing. The police had Savio's body exhumed.

The covered empty grave of Kathleen Savio, whose body was exhumed to determine her cause of death.

## Above Ground Tombs

The water table in New Orleans, Louisi-ana, is high. This means that underground water is very close to the surface. If cem-etery workers try to dig a grave, the grave will start filling with water after just a few feet. For this reason, bodies in New Orleans are entombed in vaults above ground. The vaults resemble buildings so the New Or-leans Cemetery is often called the City of the Dead.

A medical examiner performed an **autopsy** and de-termined that Savio was murdered. Drew Peterson became the primary suspect in her death. "We have been investigating this as a murder since reopening the case in November of last year [2007]," state at-torney James Glasgow said in a written statement. "We now have a scientific basis to formally and publicly classify it as such."[10] In May 2009 Peterson was arrested for the death of Kathleen Savio.

## The Catacombs of Paris

Paris, France, is home not only to the Eiffel Tower, but also to some of the most famous works of art in the world. Some of the world's most glamor-ous fashions can be found there as well as some of the fanciest restaurants. Yet, beneath this bright and bustling city lies a much darker world. In tunnels under the city rest the bones of over 6 million people. These tunnels are open to the public. For a small fee, visitors can wander amongst the dimly lit remains of the dead. Visitor Joe Kissell describes what he saw:

> What at first appeared to be walls built of small stones were in fact huge, orderly piles of human bones. Tibias and femurs by the thousands were stacked neatly, interspersed with rows of skulls, which were sometimes arranged very artistically in a cross or other pattern.[11]

In other areas the bones are simply piled in a heap. Who were these people and how did their bones end up under the city? Exactly who these people were will remain a mystery forever. There are no individual markers. However, each area of the catacombs is marked with a sign bearing the name of a cemetery.

The people whose bones rest beneath Paris died hundreds of years ago. Originally, they were buried in cemeteries in and around Paris. By the late 1700s, all the cemeteries were full. In many of these cemeteries people had been buried there for over six centuries. There were so many bodies that the ground in many of the churchyards had risen 20 feet (6m). Sometimes the graves were so shallow that bodies were easily uncovered. This was not only disturbing

In some areas of the Paris Catacombs bones are simply piled up.

to the citizens of Paris but also dangerous. Many of the people buried in these cemeteries had died of contagious diseases that could spread to the living. Something had to be done. The solution was to move the bodies to the web of underground rooms and passageways that run under Paris.

The first remains were moved in 1786. It took two years to move all the bones from that first cemetery. The bones were always transported at night in a cart covered with a black veil. The bones from other cemeteries soon followed. Today the dead under Paris outnumber those living in the city three to one.

## Floating Caskets

Hollywood Cemetery in Orange, Texas, was a mess after Hurricane Ike struck in September 2008. As the cemetery flooded, dozens of caskets floated out of their graves, some onto a nearby road.

When the floodwaters receded, the caskets needed to be reburied. However, there was a big problem. Cemetery officials needed to figure out which casket belonged in which grave. "These are somebody's somebodies," said funeral home owner Wayne Sparrow. "And it needs to be taken care of as quickly as possible."[12] Fortunately, Sparrow did not have to solve the problem on his own. The U.S. government maintains a special task force that

An uprooted casket seen in Hollywood Cemetery after Hurricane Ike.

is specially trained for just this kind of work. The Disaster Mortuary Operational Response Team (DMORT) arrived with refrigerated trucks. Caskets were loaded into these trucks by DMORT workers.

## The Body Farm

**Forensic anthropologists are learning more about how bodies decompose at The Body Farm in Tennessee. At this special research laboratory, bodies are left out in the open to decompose. Studying the bodies helps forensic anthropologists learn what happens to a body as it decomposes and how to pinpoint the time of death, which can be essential in solving crimes.**

A decaying body at The Body Farm, where bodies are studied in different stages.

Then they were taken to a lab so the bodies could be identified. Once the bodies were identified, they were taken back to the cemetery to be buried in their proper places.

## Learning About Death

In the past people did not know much about death. They relied on customs and superstitions to guide them when someone died. Today a great deal is known about how bodies decompose. **Forensic anthropologists** can identify decomposed bodies and tell when and how a person died. However, there is still a great deal we do not know about death. For many people, questions about death go far beyond what happens to the physical body. Those still living wonder what happens after death. Is there an afterlife? Do ghosts really haunt cemeteries? Maybe someday the answers will be known.

# Notes

## Chapter 2: Ancient Burials

1. Quoted in Jose Orozco, "1,000 Ancient Tombs, Unique Remains Found in Colombia," National Geographic News, May 9, 2008, http://news.nationalgeographic.com/news/2008/05/080509-colombia-tombs.html.

2. Quoted in Lothar Ledderose, *Ten Thousand Things: Module and Mass Production in Chinese Art.* NJ: Princeton University Press, 1998, pp. 51–73.

3. Quoted in *China Daily,* "30m Building Within Emperor Qin's Tomb?" *China Daily,* July 11, 2007, www.chinadaily.com.cn/ezine/2007-07/11/content_5432529.htm.

4. Quoted in Philipp Vanderberg, *The Curse of the Pharaohs.* Sevenoaks, UK: Coronet, 1975, p. 19.

5. Quoted in David Keys, "Curse (and Revenge) of the Mummy Invented by Victorian Writers," *Independent* (United Kingdom), December 31, 2000, www.independent.co.uk/news/uk/home-news/curse-of-the-mummys-tomb-invented-by-victorian-writers-626787.html.

6. Quoted in Lee Krystek, "Howard Carter and

the 'Curse of the Mummy,'" Museum of Un-natural Mystery Web site, www.unmuseum. org/mummy.htm.

## Chapter 3: Haunted Graveyards

7. Quoted in Joe Nickell, "Investigative Files Se-crets of the Voodoo Queen," *Skeptical Briefs Newsletter,* December 2001, www.csicop.org/ sb/2001-12/i-files.html.

8. Quoted in Haunted America Tours Web site, "The Top Ten Most Haunted Cemetery or Graveyards in the United States," Haunted America Tours Web site, www.hauntedameri-catours.com/hauntedcemeteries/toptenhaunt-edcemeteries.

9. Quoted in Troy Taylor, "Greenwood Cem-etery Where the Dead Still Walk," Haunted Decatur Web site, 2006, www.haunteddecatur. com/greenwood.html.

## Chapter 4: Disturbing the Dead

10. Quoted in CNN.com, "Death of Former Cop's Third Wife Ruled a Homicide," CNN. com, February 22, 2008, http://edition.cnn. com/2008/CRIME/02/21/missing.wife/in-dex.html#cnnSTCText.

11. Joe Kissell, "Paris Catacombs," Interesting Thing of the Day Web site, June 5, 2004, http://itotd.com/articles/206/paris-cata-combs.

12. Quoted in Associated Press, "Even Dead Seemed to Try to Flee Ike's Wrath," Associated Press, September 15, 2008.

# Glossary

**archaeologists:** People who study graves, buildings, tools, and other objects to learn about cultures from the past.

**artifacts:** Objects or parts of objects made by people in the past.

**autopsy:** A medical examination of a body in order to determine the cause of death.

**contagious:** Capable of being spread from one person to another either by direct or indirect contact.

**corpse:** A dead body.

**cremated:** When a dead body is burned until only ashes are left.

**deceased:** A person who is dead.

**epitaph:** Words written on a tombstone.

**exhume:** To remove a body from a grave.

**forensic anthropologists:** People who study how bodies decompose in order to determine how and when a person died.

**hallucinate:** To see or hear things that are not really there.

**resurrected:** Coming back to life after being dead.

**terra-cotta:** Brownish-red clay that is baked until hard.

**theories:** Educated guesses based on the information available.

**theorize:** To form a theory.

**veterans:** People who have served in the armed forces.

**voodoo:** A religious practice that involves magic and communication with the dead.

# For Further Exploration

## Books

Cameron Banks, *Ghostly Graveyards and Spooky Spots.* New York: Scholastic, 2004. A collection of stories about scary places in the United States. Includes photos and quizzes.

Charles George and Linda George, *The Clay Soldiers of China.* Farmington Hills, MI: KidHaven Press, 2006. This informative book discusses the discovery and excavation of the Mausoleum of the First Qin Emperor.

Timothy Pauketat and Nancy Stone Bernard, *Cahokia Mounds.* New York: Oxford University Press, 2004. This book provides a history of the mound builders and tells about explorations of the Cahokia Mounds.

Stuart L Schneider, *Ghosts in the Cemetery: A Pictorial Study.* Atglen, PA: Schiffer, 2008. This book offers photos of ghosts in cemeteries.

Michael Woods and Mary B. Woods, *The Tomb of King Tutankhamen.* Minneapolis: Twenty-First Century, 2008. This colorful and informative book tells the story of Howard Carter's discovery of King Tut's tomb. Includes sidebars, photographs, a map of the tomb, a time line, and a glossary.

## Internet Source

Barbara Gotthelf, "The Terra-Cotta Army of Emperor Qin," HighlightsKids.com, www.highlightskids.com/Stories/NonFiction/NF1298_terracotta.asp.

## Web Sites

**Field Museum** (www.fieldmuseum.org/tut/exhibition). This is the Web site of the Field Museum located in Chicago, Illinois. The museum hosted a King Tut exhibition from May 2006 to January 2007, and the Web site offers extensive information on King Tut's life, death, and tomb, including photos, room descriptions, and a wealth of information about artifacts found in the tomb.

**Haunted America Tours** (www.hauntedamericatours.com). This Web site provides information on ghosts and paranormal activity, including a wealth of stories and pictures about the most haunted graveyards in America.

**Underground Paris: A Virtual Tour** (http://triggur.org/cata). This Web site offers a room-by-room tour of the Paris catacombs with photos and text.

# Index

# Picture Credits

# About the Author

Rachel Lynette enjoys visiting cemeteries, but is happy not to be an occupant—yet. Lynette has written over 40 books for children as well as resource materials for teachers. She lives in the Seattle, Washington, area with her two children, David and Lucy, and a cat named Cosette. When she is not writing, Lynette enjoys spending time with her family and friends, traveling, reading, drawing, crocheting colorful hats, and inline skating.

## DATE DUE

|  |  |  |  |
|--|--|--|--|
|  |  |  |  |
|  |  |  |  |
|  |  |  |  |
|  |  |  |  |
|  |  |  |  |
|  |  |  |  |
|  |  |  |  |
|  |  |  |  |
|  |  |  |  |
|  |  |  |  |
|  |  |  |  |
|  |  |  |  |
|  |  |  |  |